ISBN 978-1-5282-3662-1
PIBN 10914802

This book is a reproduction of an important historical work. Forgotten Books uses state-of-the-art technology to digitally reconstruct the work, preserving the original format whilst repairing imperfections present in the aged copy. In rare cases, an imperfection in the original, such as a blemish or missing page, may be replicated in our edition. We do, however, repair the vast majority of imperfections successfully; any imperfections that remain are intentionally left to preserve the state of such historical works.

Forgotten Books is a registered trademark of FB &c Ltd.
Copyright © 2018 FB &c Ltd.
FB &c Ltd, Dalton House, 60 Windsor Avenue, London, SW19 2RR.
Company number 08720141. Registered in England and Wales.

For support please visit www.forgottenbooks.com

1 MONTH OF FREE READING

at

www.ForgottenBooks.com

By purchasing this book you are eligible for one month membership to ForgottenBooks.com, giving you unlimited access to our entire collection of over 1,000,000 titles via our web site and mobile apps.

To claim your free month visit: www.forgottenbooks.com/free914802

* Offer is valid for 45 days from date of purchase. Terms and conditions apply.

English
Français
Deutsche
Italiano
Español
Português

www.forgottenbooks.com

Mythology Photography **Fiction**
Fishing Christianity **Art** Cooking
Essays Buddhism Freemasonry
Medicine **Biology** Music **Ancient Egypt** Evolution Carpentry Physics
Dance Geology **Mathematics** Fitness
Shakespeare **Folklore** Yoga Marketing
Confidence Immortality Biographies
Poetry **Psychology** Witchcraft
Electronics Chemistry History **Law**
Accounting **Philosophy** Anthropology
Alchemy Drama Quantum Mechanics
Atheism Sexual Health **Ancient History**
Entrepreneurship Languages Sport
Paleontology Needlework Islam
Metaphysics Investment Archaeology
Parenting Statistics Criminology
Motivational

Student HANDBOOK

contents

	Page
Board of Trustees	3
Administrative Officers	4
Fire Regulations	5
Relations with the Office of Admissions and Records	6
Relations with Your College	20
Veterans Information	38
University Services for the Individual Student	42
Special Regulations	53
Index	70

UNIVERSITY OF ILLINOIS
BOARD OF TRUSTEES

Members ex Officio

William G. Stratton
  Governor of Illinois . . . . Springfield

Vernon L. Nickell, Superintendent
  of Public Instruction . . . . Springfield

Elected Members

TERM 1951 - 1957
  Wayne A. Johnston. . . . . . 135 E. 11th Pl., Chicago 5
  Herbert B. Megran . . . . . 300 W. Front St., Harvard
  Timothy W. Swain . . . . . Central National Bank Bldg.,
                                              Peoria 2

TERM 1953 - 1959
  Cushman Bissell. . . . . . 135 S. LaSalle St., Chicago 3
  Mrs. Doris S. Holt. . . . . 330 E. Sixth St., Flora
  Park Livingston . . . . . 3600 River Rd., Franklin Park

TERM 1955 - 1961
  G. Wirt Herrick . . . . . . 120-1/2 E. Main St., Clinton
  Mrs. Frances B. Watkins . . . . 5831 Blackstone Ave.,
                                              Chicago 37
  Kenny E. Williamson. . 606 Lehmann Building, Peoria 2

OFFICERS OF THE BOARD

Herbert B. Megran, President . 300 W. Front St., Harvard
Anthony J. Janata, Secretary . . . . Urbana
H. O. Farber, Comptroller . . . . Urbana
Clarence W. Weldon, Treasurer . . . . 38 S. Dearborn St.,
                                              Chicago 90

Committee on the Chicago Departments
  Mrs. Frances B. Watkins (Chairman)
  Cushman Bissell

Administrative Officers

	Room
Charles C. Caveny, Dean	360
Harold N. Cooley, Assistant to the Dean	359
Robert P. Hackett, Associate Dean, Commerce and Business Administration	27
Frederick W. Trezise, Associate Dean, Engineering Sciences	184
Harold W. Bailey, Associate Dean, Liberal Arts and Sciences	29
J. O. Jones, Director, Physical Education and Athletics	101 Gym
Warren O. Brown, Dean of Men	313
Ann Bromley, Dean of Women	313
Harold E. Temmer, Examiner and Recorder	15
Paul C. Greene, Director, Student Counseling Bureau	300
Earl B. Erskine, M.D., Director, Student Health Service	320
David K. Maxfield, Librarian	238
Robert E. Porter, Assistant to the Business Manager	352
Perry L. Smithers, Manager, Public Relations	3
David T. Wiant, Personnel Officer	Personnel Bldg.

Administrative Officers at Urbana

Lloyd Morey, President

Henning Larsen, Provost

George P. Tuttle, Director of Admissions & Records

fire regulations

Discovery of Fire. It is the responsibility of any person discovering a fire, no matter how small to REPORT IT PROMPTLY to the telephone operator and, take action to relieve the danger to loss of life. Call the operator and tell her the location of the fire by room number and/or frame number. In case of fire between the hours of 6:30 p.m. and 8 a.m. call WHitehall 4-3800.

After reporting the Fire. If there is no life hazard involved, attempt to extinguish the fire by using the auxiliary fire-fighting equipment at hand. Familiarize yourself with all exits and keep them unobstructed at all times.

relations with the office of admissions and records

1. Registration Days

   Days for registration are designated for each semester and for the summer session. A student may not register by proxy or before his assigned time. Only a student who has received his authorization card, has had his course of study approved, and has paid or arranged for his fees is registered and therefore eligible to attend classes.

2. Late Registration Procedure

A student who has not picked up his authorization card prior to the close of the regular registration period will find it in the office of the Associate Dean of his college. Such a student will be assigned to sections in his various courses by the college and departmental offices. The balance of his registration will be completed by the office of Admissions and Records in the late registration area. A former student of the University of Illinois will be charged a late registration fee if he does not complete his registration prior to the close of the regular registration period. (See "Late Registration Fee," Paragraph 4C.)

3. Registration of Listeners or Visitors

The privilege of attending classes as a listener is granted only by permission of the instructor of the class with the approval of the Associate Dean of the college concerned. Visitors are not permitted in laboratory or physical education classes. A person who visits a course as a listener is not allowed an examination for credit therein at any time.

No listener's fee is charged a registered student on a full fee schedule or a person in the permanent employ of the University. A fee of $7.50 for each course is charged all others.

The $7.50 fee for each course will be refunded if the visitor withdraws during the first 10 days of instruction in a regular semester or during the first five days of instruction in the summer session. No refund will be made if the visitor withdraws after the 10th day of instruction in a regular semester or after the 5th day of instruction in the summer session.

A listener may have library privileges by paying the $5.00 General Deposit (See Paragraph 5B, below).

4. Fees

   A. Payable at Registration. Fees assessed for any semester are due and payable in full when the student registers. For the schedule of regular University fees, see the Catalog of the Chicago Undergraduate Division.

   B. Students in Debt to the University. A student who is in debt to the University at the end of any semester for fees or charges is not permitted to register in the University again, and is not entitled to an official statement of his credits from the office of Admissions and Records, until his indebtedness has been discharged.

   C. Late Registration Fee. A student is not registered until his fees are paid. A late registration fee of $5 is charged a former student of the University of Illinois who completes his registration after the close of the regular registration period. A former student, therefore, who does not pay his fees during the regular registration period is charged the late registration fee, except during the summer session.

5. Refunds of Fees and General Deposit

If a student withdraws from the University during the first 10 days of instruction in any semester, the total amount of his tuition and fees is refunded. After the first 10 days of instruction and before the middle of the semester, a rebate of one-half of the tuition and fees will be made. After the middle of the semester, no rebate will be allowed.

The tuition and fees of a student dismissed from the University during any semester are refunded on the same basis as indicated above.

In the eight-week summer session, the total amount of tuition and fees paid is refunded on withdrawals from the University within the first five days of instruction; one-half the amount is refunded after the beginning of the 5th week of instruction.

Three items are not subject to the foregoing sliding scale of rebates:

A. **The Hospital and Medical Service Fee.** The entire Hospital and Medical Service fee is not rebated after the close of the 10th day of instruction in any semester or after the 5th day of instruction in the summer session. A student withdrawing after the period indicated may petition the Dean of Men for a pro-rata rebate of the Hospital and Medical Service fee. However, a student withdrawing after the period indicated who has paid the fee and does not request a rebate of this fee is insured for the balance of the semester, even though he is no longer attending the University.

B. **The General Deposit.** Each student must make a deposit of $5 at the time of his first registration. Such items as laboratory breakage and fines for over-due library books are chargeable against this deposit.

Whenever the balance in the general deposit fund falls below $2.50, the student will be required immediately to bring the balance up to $5 by additional deposit.

If a student withdraws from the University, any balance in his general deposit fund will be refunded to him by check, sent to his last known address, 60 days after the beginning of the semester following his withdrawal.

C. **Military Deposit.** A deposit of $10 is required of all students withdrawing military equipment. The $10 military deposit will be returned to the student, upon receipt of the military equipment, at the end of each school year.

6. **Semester Grade Reports**

A student may obtain a copy of his semester grade report by leaving at the office of Admissions and Records a self-addressed stamped envelope with his college and identification number written in the lower left corner. These reports are sent out approximately five days after the end of the examination period.

Envelopes and stamps may be obtained at the University post office, but not elsewhere in the University.

7. Transcripts of Studies and Grades

A student who has paid all his University fees is entitled to receive from the office of Admissions and Records on request, without charge, one transcript of his record. For each additional transcript a fee of 50¢ is charged. When further entries shall have been made on a student's record, he is entitled to one transcript, without charge, of his record at that stage. No charge is made at any time for transcripts sent to other divisions of the University of Illinois.

8. Change of Address or Name

Every student who, during a semester, changes his address or whose parent's address changes from that stated on his study-list should report the change at once to the office of Admissions and Records, giving both the old and new addresses and the new telephone number.

Every student who changes his name from that which appeared on his original permit to enter should report such change to the office of Admissions and Records and submit photostats of the documents authorizing the change.

9. Repetition of Courses Taken in High School

Frequently a student who has earned credit in a particular course while in high school either desires to repeat the course in college prior to proceeding with advanced courses in sequence, or is required to do so by the University because of failures in placement examinations. No college credit is allowed for such repetitions unless:

    A. Credit at the high school level in such course was not used to meet admission requirements, and

B. The student submits to the office of Admissions and Records a written request that such high school credit be dropped in order that he may receive college credit in the course when repeated here. Forms for such requests may be obtained in the office of Admissions and Records.

Exceptions:

A. No college credit may be allowed for Rhetoric 100 or Mathematics 108 under any circumstances.

B. No college credit may be allowed for Mathematics 103 to a student who presents high school credit in any two of the following:
    (1) First semester advanced algebra
    (2) Second semester advanced algebra
    (3) College algebra
    (4) Trigonometry

10. High School Credit Earned After Entrance to the University

Supplementary certificates from high school principals covering work done and examinations taken in addition to work shown on certificates previously submitted may be accepted in all cases where they refer to work done and examinations passed prior to a student's registration in the University. Having once entered the University, a student is required to obtain his credit in the examinations given by the University. Supplementary certificates relating to secondary school work done and examinations passed in the summer or at other times after his entrance to the University are not acceptable.

11. College Credit for Advanced Mathematics Taken in High School

The University of Illinois awards college credit for college algebra and for trigonometry taken at certain high schools and passed with a grade equivalent to "C" or better, provided the credit is not needed at the high school level to meet admission requirements. The office of Admissions and Records is often unable to ascertain from available transcripts the final grades for these courses and in some cases cannot ascertain at which high school the courses were taken. A student who believes that he is entitled to such credit and has not received it should check with the office of Admissions and Records.

12. How to Change Subjects or Sections (Changes in Study-Lists)

   A. A change in study-list is required: (1) to drop a course or courses in which a student is officially registered; (2) to add a course or courses; and (3) to change from one section of a course to another section of a course in which a student is officially registered.

   B. Permission to change a study-list after registration may be obtained only from the Associate Dean of the college in which the student is enrolled.

   C. Changes in study-lists should be completed and filed at the office of Admissions and Records not later than 4 p.m. of the second Monday following registration. After this date, a fee of $1 is charged for each change slip issued. The Examiner and Recorder is authorized to waive the fee for the change of study-list in cases where the change is required by a University officer.

   D. Changes in study-lists involving sectional changes only should be filed in the office of the Associate Dean of the student's college. However, such changes filed after 4 p.m. of the second Monday following registration are subject to the change fee of $1. Whenever the change fee is to be assessed it is necessary for the student to clear through the office of Admissions and Records before filing his completed change slip in the office of the Associate Dean.

E. Students already enrolled in the University will not be permitted to enter new classes after the close of the 3rd week of any regular semester. Exceptions to this rule may be made in cases in which the student is required to drop an advanced course and to add a previous course because of inability to carry the advanced course.

F. Unless otherwise noted in the change of study-list form, grades of "W" (withdrawn) will be recorded for all courses thus dropped.

13. How to Change Curriculum Within the College

(This information does not affect students in the College of Commerce, since there is only one program recorded for the lower division of that college.)

The requirements for all curricula in the College of Engineering are the same, with the exception that solid geometry is not required for architecture or architectural engineering. Changes in curricula will be made in the college office upon request at the end of any semester.

In Liberal Arts and Sciences each of the several specialized curricula has its own set of requirements so that a student who wishes to change from one curriculum to another should call at the college office and make formal request for such a change, which will be granted in cases where it is justified.

A veteran enrolled under the G.I. Bill should refer to Paragraph 41 for instructions concerning change in curriculum.

14. How To Change Colleges Within the Chicago Undergraduate Division

A. Prior to pre-registration advisement a student currently registered in one college of the Chicago Undergraduate Division who desires to change to another college of this division may effect such transfer in the following manner. The student should:

1) Go to the office of the Associate Dean of the college in which he is currently registered and secure a release from that college.

2) Present this release to the Associate Dean of the college to which he wishes to transfer.

3) If admission to the new college is approved by the Associate Dean, he will give to the student an Inter-Collegiate Transfer Permit to be taken to the office of Admissions and Records.

4) The office of Admissions and Records will then check the student's records. If the student meets the requirements for admission to the new college, transfer will be approved and an authorization card for registration in the new college will be prepared.

N.B. The inter-collegiate transfer is not complete until approved by the Examiner and Recorder, and registration in the new college will not be permitted until such approval is obtained.

Veterans attending the University under the G.I. Bill should refer to Paragraph 45 for information regarding vocational counseling which is required for veterans desiring to make an inter-collegiate transfer.

B. During pre-registration advisement and registration the student should:

1) Secure from the Associate Dean of his college an authorization card and a release.

2) Take the authorization card and release to the Associate Dean of the college to which the student wishes to transfer.

3) If the Associate Dean in (2) above approves the transfer he will make the proper notation on the authorization card and,

   a) If it is not the student's proper time to register according to the alphabetical registration schedule, the Associate Dean in (2) above will retain the authorization card and the student may pick it up at the time he is scheduled to register.

  b) If it is the student's scheduled time to register or later, the student may proceed with his registration as soon as the Associate Dean approves the transfer.

 4) If the Associate Dean in (2) above does not approve the transfer, the Associate Dean will retain the student's records and return them by mail to the Associate Dean of the student's college.

15. Admission to the University of Illinois Professional Colleges in Chicago (Medicine, Dentistry, and Pharmacy)

A student who believes he may be eligible for admission to the University of Illinois Colleges of Medicine, Dentistry, or Pharmacy should file an application for admission thereto with the Examiner and Recorder of the University of Illinois Professional Colleges in Chicago, 1853 W. Polk St., and request the office of Admissions and Records of the Chicago Undergraduate Division to forward transcripts of his records. If a student has any question about his qualifications for admission to any of these colleges, he should consult with the Associate Dean of Liberal Arts and Sciences at this Division.

16. Transfer to Urbana

  A. Students currently registered may apply for transfer to the Urbana campus by completing the Application for Transfer to Urbana. This application may be obtained at the office of Admissions and Records and should be deposited there after completion. The office of Admissions and Records will transfer the student's records upon receipt of the Application for Transfer to Urbana.

The office of Admissions and Records in Urbana will notify the student when his Application for Transfer to Urbana is approved. At this time the office of Admissions and Records in Urbana will also notify the student where and when to report for registration in Urbana.

B. A currently registered student who has applied for transfer to Urbana but is dropped at the end of the current semester by the Chicago Undergraduate Division, may petition for re-admission to the college to which he wishes to transfer. However, there is little hope that a petition under these circumstances will be approved.

C. A former Chicago Undergraduate Division student not currently registered at the Chicago Undergraduate Division who wishes to transfer to Urbana must complete an application for re-admission to the University. This application may be obtained at Window C or D, Room 15, the office of Admissions and Records, Chicago Undergraduate Division. This office will transfer the student's records at this Division to Urbana. If the student has attended another institution since leaving the Chicago Undergraduate Division, it will be the student's responsibility to have his transcripts from these institutions forwarded to the office of Admissions and Records in Urbana. A student not currently registered at the Chicago Undergraduate Division who wishes to transfer to the University in Urbana and who has been dropped for poor scholarship must file a petition for re-admission in addition to the application for re-admission; this will be forwarded to the office of Admissions and Records in Urbana.

All students, current or otherwise, who are transferring to the Urbana campus will receive a notice and/or information about their admission from the office of Admissions and Records in Urbana.

17. Transfers to Other Institutions

A student who wishes to transfer to another university or college should file with the office of Admissions and Records a written request asking that a transcript of his records be sent to the other institution and should supply full details as to the correct name and address of the institution as well as the time (present or end of current term) at which the transcript is to be prepared. Requests received by telephone will not be honored.

18. Withdrawals from the University

A student who leaves the University during any semester or summer session must officially withdraw. Otherwise the grade in each course in which he is registered will appear upon his record as "Ab" which counts as a failure. However, a student who is failing a course or courses at the time he withdraws may be required to accept the grade of "E" (failure) in such course or courses. In order to withdraw, a student should:

A. Obtain from the office of the Associate Dean of his college a clearance paper;

B. Obtain on the clearance paper the signatures of those University officers indicated by the Associate Dean;

C. Return the clearance paper to the Associate Dean for approval;

D. Deposit the clearance paper at the office of Admissions and Records.

N.B. Withdrawal is not complete until Step D is taken.

19. Withdrawal from the University to Enter into Service with the Armed Forces of the United States

If a student withdraws from the University to enter the service during the first seven weeks of instruction, he is authorized a full rebate of his tuition and fees.

If a student withdraws from the University to enter the service during the period from the 7th to the 12th week of instruction, he will receive one-half credit for all courses in which he is making a grade of "C" or better at the time of his withdrawal. Grades less than "C" will not be recorded on the student's permanent record card; but, rather, a grade of "W", indicating "withdrawal," will be recorded in this instance.

If a student withdraws from the University to enter the service after the 12th week of instruction, he will receive no rebate of tuition and fees but will receive full credit for all courses in which he was making a grade of "C" or better at the time of withdrawal.

A student withdrawing from the University to enter the service must be on active duty within 10 days of the time of withdrawal in order to benefit from the above rules. It is the responsibility of the student to present to the University proof that he was on active duty within 10 days from the time of withdrawal from the University. Usually, the most effective way to accomplish this is to have the personnel officer of the unit to which the student is assigned certify to the University the date of the student's entry to active duty.

20. Re-admission to the University

A student in any of the following categories will be required to make application for re-admission to the University before being permitted to register:

A. A student who has been dropped from the University for poor scholarship.

B. A student who has been dismissed from the University by the Sub-committee on Student Discipline.

C. A student who has formally withdrawn from the University prior to the end of the semester.

D. A student who has failed to register in the next regular semester following the one in which he was last registered. (No re-admission application is necessary for a student who completes the second (Spring) semester of any academic year and does not register in the University again until the semester commencing the following September.)

E. A student who has transferred from the Chicago Undergraduate Division to another institution may return to the University of Illinois under "former student" status at any time provided his records in the other institution are satisfactory.

Students in categories A, B, and C will be required to file petitions for re-admission. Blank forms for re-admission applications and for petitions may be obtained at the office of Admissions and Records.

Exception: Any student dropped for poor scholarship in January or June who desires immediate re-admission to the next sequential session (session beginning in February or June, respectively) is not required to submit an application for re-admission. Instead, he should consult the Dean of his college in person. Note: This exception does not apply for re-admission in September.

21. Alteration of Records

The alteration of University records, particularly study-lists, by a student is not permitted and may lead to disciplinary action. In any and all cases in which a student believes that an error has been made, he should bring it to the attention of the proper University office.

relations with your college

22. General Statement

The Chicago Undergraduate Division of the University of Illinois is made up of the three colleges of Commerce and Business Administration, Liberal Arts and Sciences, and Engineering Sciences, including both engineering and architecture, and a school of Physical Education. A student is admitted to a <u>college</u> or school in the University of Illinois. He meets <u>college</u> requirements. The <u>college</u> has final responsibility for his educational advisement and he is graduated on recommendation of the <u>college</u>. Consequently, final decision on all academic matters in the University of Illinois rests with the student's college.

23. General Requirements for Graduation

The Chicago Undergraduate Division does not offer a complete educational program for a degree, and it is not possible for a student to complete his requirements for graduation here. Nevertheless, the student will want to plan his program with a view to the requirements for graduation from his chosen curriculum. Each annual issue of the University of Illinois Bulletin on Undergraduate Study contains a section entitled "General Requirements for Graduation." The student should familiarize himself with this bulletin, as well as with the specific requirements for graduation from the college and curriculum in which he is registered.

The student should plan his program here with a view to completing the courses specifically prescribed for the first two years and meeting as many of the group and elective requirements as possible, so that he may be free to devote his years at Urbana chiefly to the advanced undergraduate courses which are not available here. Each of the colleges offers all of its students counsel on progress toward the degree in an effort to assure the maximum benefit from the time spent here.

In many fields of study, courses are offered in sequence, and failure to start such sequences at the proper time or to continue them as prescribed may result in the student's being unable to complete the requirements for graduation within the normal time.

24. Residence Requirements for Graduation

A bachelor's degree is conferred on a student who completes satisfactorily a curriculum in one of the colleges or schools of the University, doing either the first three years (not less than ninety semester hours) or the last year (not less than thirty semester hours) of work in residence. Until such time as the Chicago Undergraduate Division is authorized to grant degrees, students from that division must complete either the junior or senior year (thirty semester hours) on the Urbana campus.

25. Pre-Registration Advisement

During a period immediately prior to registration in each semester, the colleges of Commerce and Business Administration and Liberal Arts and Sciences offer to their returning students assistance in the planning of programs of study for the ensuing semester. This allows the student to discuss with an advisor his selection of courses, both for that semester and over a longer period, thus eliminating this step in the regular registration process. The student will find that his problems can be given more thorough consideration if he will use the opportunity for the preparation of his study-list rather than wait until the regular registration days.

The College of Engineering has a permanent advisory system which carries on counseling at the convenience of the student and the advisor throughout the entire year. Each new student in Engineering is assigned an advisor soon after the beginning of the semester.

Physical Education does not offer a regular pre-registration advisement program. It has an advisory plan that operates continuously.

26. Scholastic Requirements

The scholastic progress of a student is the concern of the Associate Dean of his college or the Director of his school and unsatisfactory work will subject the student to action by the Associate Dean or Director. This may take the form of a warning, a period of probation, or, if his work is very poor, of being dropped from the college or school for scholastic deficiencies. The following minimum scholarship requirements are in effect.

- A. Probation: If at the end of any semester a student's average for that semester falls below 3.0, he is placed on probation for the following semester.

- B. Continuance in the University: If at the end of a semester on probation a student's average for that semester is 3.0 or above, he is removed from probation. If his average is below 3.0 for that semester, he is dropped from the University for poor scholarship. This is a minimum and does not abrogate the authority of any school or college to set higher minimum requirements.

C. Graduation Requirement: A minimum average of 3.0 is required for graduation from all curricula for students entering the University after October 1, 1947.

27. Additional Scholastic Requirements for Individual Colleges

   A. Commerce and Business Administration

   1) Without the permission of the Associate Dean of the college, a student on probation may not register for more than 12 credit hours, exclusive of physical education and military science.

   2) A student, whether or not previously on probation, will be dropped from the University if he fails in any semester to pass at least six credit hours (three credit hours in the eight-week summer session) of work for which he is regularly registered, exclusive of physical education and military science.

   3) No grades except those earned at the University of Illinois shall be considered in the application of the probation and drop rules.

   4) A student must have an average of 3.0 or above for all courses counted toward graduation whether taken at the University of Illinois or elsewhere.

   B. Engineering Sciences

   1) Grade Point System:
      The grade point system is used in determining the student's scholastic status in regard to the

probation and drop rules and in meeting graduation requirements. (See Paragraph 28-A, below)

In computing grade points in the application of the probation and drop rules, all courses which the student has taken count, excepting Math. 108 and Rhet. 100. Math. 106, 103, 103x, 112, and 114 do not count toward graduation.

2) Probation Rules:

The effect of "probation" is to exclude a student from all college or University extra-curricular activities and to warn him that he is subject to the operation of the "drop" rules at the end of the semester in which the probation applies if his scholastic achievement does not improve.

a) A student in the College of Engineering is placed on probation for the next semester in which he is registered if he fails to pass eleven hours of work in any semester; or, if being registered for less than eleven hours, he does not pass all his work, — military, physical education, and all non-credit courses except Math. 108 and Rhet. 100.

b) A student who does not make a 3.0 point average in the credit hours in which he is registered in any semester will be placed on probation for the next semester in which he is registered. Math. 108 and Rhet. 100 do not yield grade points, nor count as credit hours in the application of this rule.

c) A student will be placed on probation for the next semester in which he is registered who after he has passed 60 credit hours, taken at the University of Illinois, exclusive of physical education and military, and courses passed by proficiency and special examination, fails to secure a 3.0 average on the total hours passed at the University, not counting the hours and/or grade points in the excluded courses.

d) A student may be placed on probation at any time when, in the judgment of the dean of the college, his scholastic record warrants such action.

3) Drop Rules:

a) A student in the college of engineering who has been placed on probation under any rule or action of the college will be dropped at the end of his succeeding semester of registration:

1) If he does not pass eleven hours of work including physical education, military, and all non-credit courses except Math. 108 and Rhet. 100; or, if being registered in less than eleven hours, he does not pass all of his work, and

2) If his grade point average for the succeeding semester falls below 3.0 in the credit hours in which he is registered, — Math. 108 and Rhet. 100 not yielding grade points, and

3) If having been placed on probation under Rule 3 of the Probation rules, he fails to secure a grade average at least 3.5 for each succeeding semester until his average, exclusive of military and physical education and courses passed by proficiency and special examinations, has reached the minimum graduation level of 3.0.

b) A student will be dropped who does not pass six hours of work in any semester; exclusive of Math. 108 and Rhet. 100; or, if being registered in less than six hours, he does not pass all of his work.

4) Attendance Rules:

Students must attend all classes in which they are registered unless officially withdrawn by the dean of the college.

All work missed by reason of absence must be made up.

There are no prescribed limits on the number of absences permitted but excessive "cutting" of classes will make the student liable to disciplinary action.

C. <u>Liberal Arts and Sciences.</u>

1) Freshmen.

   a) A first semester freshman must pass six hours of credit with grades of "C" or better ("C" average for six hours not accepted); otherwise, he will be dropped and denied re-admission for at least two semesters.

   b) If six hours of credit with grades of "C" or higher have been passed but the student does not have a "C" average, he will then continue on a 3.25 average probation for the following semester. Should this probation be violated, the student will be dropped for at least two semesters. If the probation is satisfied and the total average to date approaches a 3.0 average, then continuation may be possible under probationary status. (In order to meet the 3.25 average, a student must have at least one-fourth of the hours of work of "B" grade and the remaining three-fourths of "C" grade. If the 3.25 average has been obtained from "A" and "D" grades, the student may be dropped because of an excess number of hours of "D" at the end of the second semester.)

   c) Rhetoric 100, Mathematics 103 (if taken for no credit), Mathematics 108, and physical education will play no part in determining probation and drop status.

2) Sophomores.

a) A student who has more than 27 hours of credit and fewer than 56 but who does not have a 3.0 average will be on probation.

b) If the cumulative average is not 3.0 by the time the student accumulates 56 hours of credit, he will be dropped from the college for at least one semester.

3) Transfer Students.

A student who transfers to this college from another college or school will be subject to the same regulations and treated as if he had been a student in this college.

4) Pre-Professional Curricula.

A student who has not been able to maintain the scholastic requirements in a pre-professional curriculum and who has changed to the general curriculum will be governed by the above regulations.

5) General Regulations.

A 3.0 average is required for graduation from this college, and not more than one-fourth of the semester hours presented for a degree may be of "D" grade. Therefore, if, in the judgment of the Associate Dean, a student is not making satisfactory progress toward his degree, he may be placed on probation or dropped at the end of any semester. While on probation, a student must carry at least 12 hours of academic work.

The student should realize that to produce the minimum acceptable average of 3.0, each hour of "E" grade must be balanced by one hour of "A" grade or two hours of "B" grade, and each hour of "D" grade must be balanced by one hour of "B" grade.

In computing the grade-point average for graduation, all work which may be counted toward the degree will be counted even though the number of hours exceeds the minimum number required. Work which cannot be counted toward graduation (as, for example, 15 hours in engineering courses where only 10 may be counted toward graduation) will not be used in computing the grade-point average.

D. Physical Education.

1) Without the permission of the Director, a student on probation may not register for more than 12 credit hours.

2) A student, whether or not previously on probation, will be dropped from the University if he fails in any semester to pass at least six credit hours (three credit hours in the eight-week summer session) of work for which he is regularly registered.

3) A student will be placed on probation if at the end of any semester he fails to make a 3.0 average.

4) A student must have a grade average of 3.5 in order to qualify for student teaching.

28. Grades

A. Significance of Grades. The grading system is as follows: "A," excellent; "B," good; "C," fair; "D," poor but passing; "E," failure. In computing averages, the number of hours of credit for a course is multiplied by the following points; 5 for an "A"; 4 for a "B"; 3 for a "C"; 2 for a "D"; and 1 for an "E." The products thus obtained are added and the total divided by the total number of hours to obtain the average. The grade of "Ab" is used to indicate the absence of a student from a final examination without an excuse and counts as "E." "Ex" indicates that a student has been excused from a final examination. "W" is used to indicate that a student has withdrawn from a course without prejudice.

B. Honors. Honors Day is observed annually at the Chicago Undergraduate Division as an occasion upon which the University of Illinois gives official, public recognition to those students who excel in scholarship. The following honors are awarded:

1) Class Honors. A student in the upper 10 per cent of his class in his college is awarded class honors and is entitled to have his name printed on the convocation program in recognition of his high scholarship, provided that no student shall be included whose average is below "B" or who has a failure in any course on his record. A student who receives class honors three times is entitled to wear the scholarship key.

2) College Honors. A student in the upper three per cent of the sophomore or higher class in his college is awarded college honors in recognition of his superior scholarship. A student who receives college honors two times is entitled to wear the scholarship key.

C. Scholastic Honoraries.

1) Alpha Lambda Delta. A national honorary society for freshman women. In order to qualify for membership a student must carry at least 15 hours of academic work per semester and have at least a 4.5 average. A student may also qualify for membership during her second semester enrollment if she has carried 15 hours each semester and the combined average for the first two semesters of the college enrollment is 4.5 or better.

2) Phi Eta Sigma. A national honorary society for freshman men. Requirements for membership

are a 4.5 or better average for a minimum of 12 hours credit, or a 4.5 average during the first year of enrollment and a minimum of 24 hours credit. Phi Eta Sigma is established to promote a higher standard of learning and to encourage high scholastic achievement among freshman men in the University.

D. **Mid-Term Grade Reports.** Reports are required each semester from each instructor on the work of all students. Students in Commerce may obtain mid-term grades by calling in person at the college office. Engineering and Physical Education students may obtain mid-term grades from their faculty advisors, and students in Liberal Arts may obtain them from their instructors.

29. Repeating a Course

    A. **For Students in Commerce.** If a student is permitted by the Associate Dean to repeat a course for which he has received credit either by class work at the University or by advanced standing allowed for work done elsewhere, he forfeits his credit, and the grade given at the end of the repetition becomes the official grade.

    B. **For Students in Engineering.** Registration in any course for which a grade has previously been received cancels the former grade. The grade received at the end of the second registration becomes the official grade, with the following exception: in case of freshman courses, the first grade stands in computing graduation requirements unless the second grade is lower. If the second grade is "E," "Ab," or "W" all credit in the course is canceled. In the case of failure (grade of "E" or "Ab"), the grade obtained upon repetition replaces the failing grade in all courses.

    C. **For Students in Liberal Arts.** If a student is permitted by the Associate Dean to repeat a course in which he has credit, the study-list will be endorsed "for no credit," and the grade earned will not be counted in determining grade-point average under probation or drop rules, or for graduation, but the grade appears on the official transcript. The student must do all of the work in the course and must take the final examination. In computing the cumulative grade-point average at the end of any one semester or for graduation, both a failing grade ("E" or "Ab") and a passing grade on repetition of the course will be counted; it is not possible to remove a failing grade by repetition of the course.

D. For Students in Physical Education. If a student is permitted by the Director to repeat a course for which he has received credit either by class work at the University or by advanced standing allowed for work done elsewhere, he forfeits his credit, and the grade given at the end of the repetition becomes the official grade.

30. Correspondence Courses

A student registered for courses in residence at the University of Illinois or at any other college or university will not be permitted to enroll in correspondence courses, except upon the recommendation of the Dean of his college and with the approval of the Dean of University Extension. If a student has enrolled for correspondence study and before completion registers for study in residence at this or at any other institution of college grade, he will be required to secure the consent of the Dean of his college before continuing the correspondence studies for which he is enrolled. A student who is under "drop" status may register for correspondence courses only with the approval in writing of the Dean of the college from which he has been dropped. A college student who is temporarily not in residence at the University has an opportunity to continue his progress toward graduation by means of home study in the courses listed in the Correspondence Study bulletin. This bulletin may be obtained by writing to the Dean of University Extension, Urbana, Illinois.

After matriculation, a student may count, toward his degree, as much as 60 semester hours of credit earned in correspondence study in subjects passed with grades of "C" or higher, under the following conditions: (1) if he completes all the remaining requirements for the degree in residence at the University; or (2) if he presents acceptable residence credit for work done elsewhere and completes the requirements needed for his degree in residence at the University. In all such cases the senior year (of not less than 30 semester hours) must be done in residence at the University.

A student who has earned three years of residence credit at the University may do his senior year in correspondence study, subject to meeting all the requirements for his degree as announced by his college or school.

31. English Requirement

All students entering the University as freshmen direct from secondary school are required to take a placement test in rhetoric. Those who fail to pass this test must make up the deficiency by tutoring, correspondence study, or by passing Rhetoric 100 (a non-credit course meeting three hours each week). A student who fails to pass the placement test or Rhetoric 100 by the beginning of his third semester must withdraw until he does pass.

A satisfactory proficiency in the use of written English is a requirement for all undergraduate degrees awarded by the Urbana divisions of the University. In order to assure such proficiency, students who receive grades of "C" or "D" in Rhetoric 102, or its equivalent, are required to take an English qualifying examination before graduating. Those who fail to pass the qualifying examination are required to pass an extra semester course in rhetoric (Rhetoric 200).

32. Examinations

    A. Semester Examinations. Final examinations are given at the close of each semester in all courses except those in which they are impracticable.

A student who is absent from a semester examination for satisfactory reasons may be excused only by the Associate Dean of the college and examined by the instructor at his convenience. If the semester examination cannot be taken by the close of the examination period, the instructor will report the grade of the student as "Ex" (excused), and if it is not removed during the first semester that a student completes following the assigning of such a grade, the grade automatically becomes a grade of "E." The "Ex" grade can be removed by the student by any of the following means:

1) By examination prior to the end of the next semester which the student completes in residence. The student will make arrangements for the examination with the instructor concerned.

2) By re-registering in the course in which the "Ex" grade was given during the next semester of his residence and by successfully completing the course. The grade earned on successfully completing the repeated course becomes the grade for the course and the "Ex" grade is removed.

   a) If the student withdraws from the course, then he may remove the "Ex" grade as indicated in (1) above.

   b) If the student withdraws from the University, then the "Ex" grade stands until the next semester the student spends in residence and the above applies.

It should be emphasized that unless the "Ex" grade is removed prior to the end of the first semester that a student completes following the giving of the "Ex" grade, this grade becomes an automatic failure.

B. Proficiency Examinations. Proficiency examinations, analagous to the regular semester examinations, are available in all courses normally open to freshmen and sophomores. There is no fee charged for these examinations. A student who passes a proficiency examination is given credit toward graduation, provided that this does not duplicate credit counted for his admission to the University and that the course is acceptable to his curriculum. The grade in proficiency examinations is "pass" or "not pass," but no student is given a grade of "pass" unless he has made at least "C" in the examination. No official record is made of failures in these examinations.

Proficiency examinations are given under the following restrictions: (1) They may be taken only by persons who are in residence. (2) They may not be taken by students who have received credit for more than one semester of work in the subject in advance of the course in which the examination is requested. (3) They may not be taken to raise grades or to remove failures in courses.

C. Special Examinations. Special examinations may be taken only in courses failed ("E" or "Ab") at the University of Illinois. A special examination in a course failed should be taken before the end of the next semester in which the student is registered following such failure. This examination may be had only upon the recommendation of the head of the department or the chairman of the division concerned, with the approval of the Associate Dean of the college in which the student is enrolled. Special examinations are reported as "passed" or "not passed," but no student is given a grade of "pass" unless he has made at least "C" in the examination. Grades earned in special examinations do not enter into any computation of averages, but credit earned by special examinations may be counted toward graduation. Requests for special examinations should be initiated at the office of the head of the department or chairman of the division concerned. For each special examination a fee of $5 must be paid in advance.

Additional provisions with reference to special examinations are as follows:

1) No special examinations may be given during the period beginning 10 days before and continuing for 10 days after each final examination period, except that special examinations may be given on and after the first Friday of the second semester.

2) A student who has completed the work of a semester is considered to be still under registration for the purposes of this rule for 15 days after the close of the final examination period, except that a student who has completed the work of the second semester and is not registered in the summer session is considered to be still under registration for the purposes of this rule up to the end of the registration period of the fall semester. (Students who have been dropped from the University are not eligible to take special examinations.)

3) The Recorder is authorized to issue permits for special examinations to persons who are not registered in the University at the time but who are candidates for degrees at the close of the college year in which the examination is to be given and who have no more than 10 semester hours to complete for their degrees.

4) No student who has attended the University of Illinois will be permitted to take for credit at the University the examinations conducted by the University in Chicago primarily for candidates for admission to the State Bar Examination. In no case will credit be allowed toward the degree for these college examinations given by the University in Chicago until the applicant for such credit has earned in residence at the University an amount of credit equal to that earned through examinations.

33. Absences

   A. <u>Class Absences</u>. All absences of undergraduates from classes are reported to the office of the Dean of Students. A record of absences is kept for informational purposes. Explanation of absences over extended periods may be called for by the Dean of Men and Dean of Women for the purpose of information. A student absent due to a quarantinable disease must report to the Health Service before returning to classes.

   No absences from class are "excused" but are to be explained to the instructor on request.

   General regulations touching absences from class by groups, as athletic teams, musical organizations, and the like, are determined by the Senate, acting through the Faculty Committee on Student Affairs, and enforced in the particular case by the Sub-Committee on Student Discipline. Group absences for field trips in connection with academic work must be reported to the offices of the Dean of Men and Dean of Women. Forms for petitions for group absences are available at the University Business office and the office of the Dean of Students.

   B. <u>Dropping for Absences</u>. When an instructor reports that a student's absences are impairing his class standing, the Associate Dean of the student's college may require the student to withdraw from the course with a grade of "W" or "E." If the grade of "E" is given, such failure may not be removed by special examination.

   In the College of Commerce, if a student is dropped from more than one-third of his work for absences, he will be withdrawn from the University.

   C. <u>Special Discipline for Repeated Absence</u>. If the repeated absence of any student from classes seems to the Associate Dean of the college a matter requiring discipline, the case will be reported to the Sub-Committee on Discipline for action.

34. Physical Education Requirements

Men and women entering the University with less than sixty semester hours of credit are required to secure four semesters of credit in physical education including the amount transferred. Those entering with sixty or more semester hours are exempt from the requirement in physical education.

Physical education may be deferred only by written request through the Physical Education department which will make recommendation to the associate dean of the student's college. Final authority rests with the associate dean.

35. Military

The Chicago Undergraduate Division offers its male students the opportunity to complete the two-year basic ROTC course and the first year of the advanced course in military science and tactics. The enrollment and participation are voluntary. Students who successfully complete the first two years and transfer to Urbana are considered for the advanced course on an equal basis with applicants from any other basic course. Students who have had three years of high school ROTC may apply for admission to the sophomore year of the basic ROTC course. The two branches of service offered are Engineers and Infantry. Uniforms and necessary texts and equipment are provided by the University. Refer to Paragraph 5, Section C, for information on the military deposit.

A male student who transfers to Urbana from the Chicago Undergraduate Division with junior standing is not required to register in military science and tactics at Urbana. A male student who transfers to Urbana from the Chicago Undergraduate Division with less than junior standing is required to take two years of basic military science and tactics, unless this requirement is waived by the proper authorities.

36. Hygiene

Personal and Environmental Hygiene is required of all students during their first year of residence.

The hygiene requirement for graduation does not apply to transfer students who enter the University of Illinois with sophomore standing.

veterans' information

37. Training Records — University Veterans Office

The Veterans Office, located in Room 15, keeps all training records for students attending the Chicago Undergraduate Division under the G.I. Bill (P.L. 346), the Korean G.I. Bill (P.L. 550), and the Vocational Rehabilitation Training Act (P.L. 16 and P.L. 894). All questions regarding Certificates of Eligibility, training, subsistence, dependency, and transfer of school under all these bills should be referred to this office.

38. Veterans' Counselor

The Veterans' Counselor, located in the Dean of Men's office, Room 313C, gives special attention to the particular problems of veterans just beginning or continuing their education.

39. Claims and Benefits — Illinois Veterans' Commission

Veterans having questions concerning government insurance, state bonus, subsistence check tracers, dependency claims, etc., may report to the University Veterans Office in Room 15, which will assist them whenever possible or refer them to the Chicago office of the Illinois Veterans Commission, a state service organization.

40. Public Laws 16 and 894

Veterans Administration training officers hold periodic conferences with veterans in training under Public Laws 16 and 894, to assist these veterans with any problems concerning their education or future benefits. Each Public Law 16 and Public Law 894 veteran is notified directly by his training officer and the meeting is held in Room 15.

41. Change of Study Program

   A. Subsistence

      The Veterans Administration is informed by the University of courses added or dropped which affect the amount of subsistence payments. Under P.L. 550, 14 or more credit hours per semester entitle a veteran to full subsistence. Under P.L. 346, 12 or more credit hours per semester entitle a veteran to full subsistence. Payments are pro-rated for programs of less than these amounts.

   B. Books

      Books issued to veterans using P.L. 346 must be returned to the University Bookstore if the course is dropped later.

42. Books and Supplies

Veterans using Public Law 550 must pay for their books and supplies.

Such books, supplies, and equipment as are required of all students registered in any given course will be issued to veterans using Public Law 346, 16, or 894. The material must be returned to the University Bookstore if the veteran withdraws from the University before the end of the semester.

43. Withdrawal During the Semester

A veteran withdrawing from the University before the end of a semester should follow instructions in "Withdrawal from the University." This is important in protecting G.I. benefits by keeping records complete and correct. It will also help to avoid overpayment of subsistence allowance.

44. Scholastic Requirements

A student using Public Law 346 who is dropped from the University because of poor scholarship will lose his G.I. Bill unless he can enter another school for the next regular semester. This approval must be requested before the end of the semester preceding the change.

If a student using Public Law 550, whose delimiting date has passed, is dropped from the University because of poor scholarship, he must resume his training by the end of twelve months or lose his G.I. Bill.

Official Veterans Administration forms for requesting any change of course or school are available at the Veterans Office.

45. Transfers

A veteran student using Public Law 550, transferring to Urbana or to other schools must request the Veterans Office to complete a Change of Place of Training Form. This form must be presented to the Veterans Administration in order to receive a Certificate of Eligibility authorizing training at the new school. If a student transferring to another school plans to change his major field or final objective he should apply early enough to allow time for counseling by the Veterans Administration.

Veterans using Public Law 346 do not need a new authorization to transfer to Urbana but they must have a new authorization for any other school. This application for transfer must be received by the Veterans Administration before the student completes his last semester in this University. All forms are available in Room 15.

46. Inter-College Transfers or Change of Educational Objective

Any change in an educational objective requires a new Certificate of Eligibility from the Veterans Administration. Certain inter-college transfers not involving a change of objective may be approved within the University. Students intending to make a change should request the necessary forms from the Veterans Office prior to the end of the semester preceding the change.

university services for the individual student

47. Dean of Students

The Dean of Students is largely responsible for the welfare of the student outside the classroom. He is charged with the direction, supervision, and co-ordination of the University agencies which are active in the guidance of students in extra-curricular activities, and he serves as advisor to foreign students. Student activities of an extra-curricular nature are supervised by the Committee on Student Affairs.

The principal assistants to the Dean of Students are the Dean of Men, the Dean of Women, and the assistant to the Dean of Men. These individuals serve as general advisors to whom students may turn for assistance and advice. These advisors help with problems of personal adjustment to college life, how to find part-time employment, how to budget expenses and time, what loan funds and scholarships are available, questions about student activities, and interpretation of University rules. The Dean of Men, the Dean of Women, and the assistant are available for individual conferences with students daily.

48. Student Health and Welfare Services

   A. Health Service. The University maintains a Health Service for students to protect their physical and mental health, to control communicable diseases among them, and to teach them the essentials of healthful living. Health Service staff members conduct courses in hygiene, conduct physical examinations, make sanitary inspections, and counsel students about individual health problems.

   These functions are primarily educational and preventive, and the Health Service staff does not assume responsibility for the care of students beyond giving medical advice, emergency treatment, and immunizing inoculations. Inoculations for smallpox, tetanus, diphtheria, influenza, and typhoid fever are available to students, faculty, and non-academic personnel. Annual physical examinations are required of all students.

   Health record forms containing the results of physical examinations and immunization treatments are kept during the period of a student's enrollment.

A sheet prepared by the Physical Education department showing physical improvement is likewise a part of the record. A copy of this health record is available to any student.

The Health Service is located at the east end of Navy Pier on the third floor. Hours are from 8 a.m. to 6 p.m. weekdays during the school session.

The facilities of the University of Illinois Chicago Professional Colleges are available to the Health Service in such cases as are deemed to be the responsibility of the Health Service toward Undergraduate Division students. Such facilities, however, are available only when requested by the Director of the Chicago Undergraduate Division Student Health Service.

B. Hospital and Medical Insurance Benefits. The Hospital and Medical Service insurance, for which a fee is charged each student at each registration, is a health insurance plan administered by the Office of the Dean of Men.

This insurance plan provides substantial payments toward hospital residence, miscellaneous hospital services, physician's charges, surgical operation expenses, consultant's expenses, ambulance expenses, out-patient expenses, catastrophic expenses and maternity expense, providing the insured, on account of injuries or disease, is confined to a hospital or ill at home and unable to attend his regular classes.

Before claims are processed and claim payments made, the student must have reported the injury or illness to the Dean of Men within 20 days after the date of the accident causing such injury or within 10 days after the commencement of disability from the illness. Upon receipt of the above information, the Office of the Dean of Men will furnish to the insured such forms as are usually required for filing a claim. Two additional steps must be taken by the insured in order to report a claim to the Dean of

Men: (1) Have filled out by the hospital and/or physician the blue claim form that was mailed to you; (2) file an itemized statement from the hospital and/or doctor's charges for the services rendered during the hospital confinement period or the time confined at home. Claim forms and detailed information regarding the insurance may be obtained in the Office of the Dean of Men.

Although all students are required to pay the hospital and medical service fee, any student participating in an insurance plan providing the same benefits may petition for a refund by contacting the Office of the Dean of Men within the first ten days of instruction during a regular semester or within the first five days of instruction during the summer session.

49. Scholarships and Financial Aid

   A. Scholarships. A number of scholarship funds have been established by individuals, organizations, and the State of Illinois. Scholarship awards vary in amount as do the eligibility requirements. Information concerning scholarships for undergraduate students is contained in a booklet which is available at the Veterans' Benefits office, Room 15, and the office of the Dean of Students, Room 313.

   Most of the scholarships exempt students from tuition charges at either Urbana or the Chicago Undergraduate Division. Notice of the scholarship award must be on file prior to registration at the division of the University the student plans to attend.

   B. Student Loan Funds. Loan funds are of two general classes: (1) emergency loan funds, and (2) long-term loan funds. Emergency loan funds are available in small amounts for short periods only. Long-term loan funds are for larger loans and may be carried for a longer time. The long-term loans ordinarily are not available to students during their first year in the University. Application blanks and detailed information regarding loan funds may be obtained from the office of the Dean of Men, Room 313.

C. Student Employment. For students who find it necessary to earn a portion of their expenses, a limited number of part-time jobs are available in various University offices and departments as well as with industries and business establishments in Chicago. Students who desire a part-time position should file an application with the office of the Dean of Men, Room 313.

50. Student Counseling Bureau

The Bureau helps registered and prospective students to make effective use of the University's resources. It assists students in meeting their individual needs and in coping with a wide variety of problems that occur in the course of college life.

Students and prospective students are aided in making decisions as to which college or educational program to select in the University. Help is given in arriving at suitable vocational choices. Counselors aid in analyzing and relieving difficulties in studying. They also aid students in removing stumbling blocks to overall personal growth and success, and in realizing their potential for fuller and more rapid development.

A. Individual Counseling. Students who feel they have the above needs or problems, and others who for any reason find they are not fully profiting from college life, are invited to talk over their situation with a professionally-trained counselor. Interview schedules are flexible, and students usually can arrange for as much counseling time as they need. Professional aid can play a large part in helping students to do improved problem-solving, to do more effective planning, to lead fuller lives academically and socially, and to derive maximum benefit from their college careers.

B. <u>Test Services</u>. Tests of special aptitudes, vocational and scholastic interests, and of personal-social adjustment may be taken by individual arrangement with a counselor. These counseling aids frequently prove valuable in self-evaluation and in making plans appropriate to one's abilities, aptitudes and life-situation.

The Bureau also has arranged to give guidance tests for all freshman students, and to give each student an opportunity to review test ratings with a counselor as these bear on self-evaluation and planning. Test scores show relationships between one's own high and low points of interest and aptitude, and they also give a basis for comparing oneself with other students. Other tests and interest inventories are available to all students at the Chicago Undergraduate Division.

C. <u>Group Counseling</u>. Group counseling sessions are available at a number of times throughout the year, including the summer. It is intended for students who have found special problems of adjustment to their college work, as well as for those who are making good progress but feel a need to increase their personal efficiency so as to lead fuller lives in and out of college. Groups are kept small, and they usually meet twice a week. Group work is geared in with individual counseling where appropriate. Some of the groups deal with a variety of common student problems. Other groups give more specialized attention to such problems as: reading for different purposes, improving powers of concentration, aiding the ability to remember, improving preparation for course examinations, taking more usable notes, organizing one's time more efficiently, and learning a variety of methods for studying different courses and course-materials. A personal interview before admission to this program helps one in selecting a group appropriate to individual needs.

D. Location. The Student Counseling Bureau occupies a suite of rooms on the third floor, near the lake end of the Pier. It is near a student lounge on the same floor, and adjacent to the offices of the student deans and the Health Service.

Receptionists are in attendance to aid students in making and meeting appointments. Additional information may be obtained at the reception desk, or by calling Ext. 115 at WHitehall 4-3800.

51. Speech Correction Program

The Speech Clinic is maintained by the University to help students in correcting speech defects. Students with special problems, such as poor voice quality, defective articulation, and stuttering, should go to the Student Counseling Bureau in Room 300 for an appointment with the Director of the Speech Clinic. Those applying for aid are tested to determine the type and extent of their speech difficulties. A program of corrective exercises is then prescribed, with supervised practice periods one or two hours a week. A slight fee is sometimes required for making a speech recording, but otherwise the service is provided without charge.

52. Library Services.

To describe the Library's facilities and services, which compare favorably with libraries of four-year colleges all over the country, and to explain how students may use the Library efficiently for their studies and extra-curricular activities, the library staff has prepared the U.I.C. Undergraduate Library Handbook. All freshmen will find it desirable to purchase personal copies from the University Bookstore, since this booklet is a required text for both Rhet. 101 and Rhet. 102. It should also be kept handy for reference use throughout the time a student attends classes at the Pier. A summary of the Library's rules and regulations follows.

A. Library Hours. The Main Reading Room, the Reserve Book Station, and the Fine Arts Reading Room are open 8:30 to 4:30 Monday through Friday and are closed on Saturdays. All library departments are closed on University holidays, and only the Main Reading Room is open during intersession and vacation periods.

B. Identification Cards and Circulation Records. All students must show their University Identification Cards whenever they withdraw library materials for use outside the reading rooms, or withdraw reserve books, etc. for use within the reading rooms. No library materials may be removed from the various library departments unless the necessary record cards have been properly signed. Students leaving library departments must be prepared to show all books, pamphlets, and periodicals which they are carrying (whether contained in brief cases or otherwise) to the attendants, upon request.

C. Open Shelf Books. With the exception of reference books and periodicals, open shelf books may usually be borrowed for home use for a period of two weeks. They may be renewed (with some exceptions) for another two weeks with the understanding that all renewed books are subject to immediate recall if needed by other readers. Students are fined five cents a day for keeping open shelf books overtime. Individuals found to be withdrawing unreasonable quantities of books will be asked to return the number considered excessive. Other library materials may be subject to various special loan conditions.

D. Reserve Books. The withdrawal periods for reserve books depend upon various needs and conditions. Most reserve books must be used in the various reading rooms, or on the Pier, until the overnight check-out time. Some reserve books may be borrowed to take home for periods varying from three days to one week. The fine for the late return of a reserve book is 25 cents for the first hour and five cents for each additional hour.

E. Reference Books and Bound Periodicals. Almost all reference books and periodicals are freely available on open shelves. However, a few selected current issues of magazines and journals are kept "on reserve" at the circulation counters. Reference books and periodicals must be used within the reading rooms.

F. Return of Library Materials. All library materials which have been borrowed must be returned to the same circulation counters from which they were checked out, and must be returned at or before the date and/or time specified at the time of loan. Materials used within the reading rooms, including books consulted in the stacks, should be left on the reading room tables.

G. Student Book Fines and Lost Books. Fines for overdue books and charges for lost books are deducted from the General Deposit paid by each student at registration time. Students must fill out and sign a General Deposit Account Card for each such fine or charge. When necessary, the Library may fill out a General Deposit Account Card for s student in absentia. Lost books should be reported immediately to avoid the building up of excessive fines, and if not found after a reasonable period, the loser will be charged for them.

H. Mutilated Books. Deliberate mutilation of library materials is both a State offense, and a matter for University disciplinary action. Books accidentally damaged should be reported and paid for at once.

I. Main Reading Room No Thoroughfare. The stairway at the east end of the Main Reading Room, and the fire-doors connecting with the drafting rooms in the building east of the Main Reading Room, are to be used only in times of emergency such as fire.

J. Quiet. Since the library is intended for purposes of reading and serious study, quiet must be observed at all times in the various departments.

K. No Smoking. Smoking is not permitted in the Main Reading Room, Fine Arts Reading Room, or the Reserve Book Station.

L. Conduct and Discipline. Failure to maintain suitable standards of conduct in the Main Reading Room, the Fine Arts Reading Room, or the Reserve Book Station, or failure to observe these regulations, will lead to action by the Sub-Committee on Student Discipline, after due warning by library staff members.

53. Bookstore

The University bookstore has been established by the University of Illinois and is owned and operated by the University, as a service to the students.

The main purpose and object of the University bookstore is to provide a source of supply to students for all necessary texts and supplies as required by the various courses being offered at the University's Undergraduate Division.

The bookstore is located in Room 87. It is open daily Monday through Friday from 8:30 a.m. to 4:30 p.m. and on Saturday during registration.

54. Food Service

A University-operated cafeteria located at the east end of the Pier serves breakfasts and lunches. Two Snack Bars, one located in the Main Lounge at the west end of the Pier and the other in the east end cafeteria, serve light lunches and provide soda fountain service. Students are requested to return their trays to the dish room in the east end cafeteria.

55. Informational Services

A. Information Desk. The University maintains an information desk for the convenience of students and visitors. General information pertaining to the Chicago Undergraduate Division and to the University of Illinois, in addition to the student's home addresses and telephone numbers and available housing, may be secured from the receptionist.

B. <u>Bulletin Boards.</u> There are five glass-covered bulletin boards reserved for student organizations publicity. Before material is posted, the student shall deliver same to the Office of the Dean of Students where the approved stamp and the initials of the dean may be applied to the material which is then forwarded to the Physical Plant department for posting in the glass-covered student activities bulletin boards. The individual departmental bulletin boards usually located on the wall immediately outside the doorway to the departmental offices are not to be used for student activities unless approved by the department concerned. Posters advertising regular club and organization events should be $8\frac{1}{2}$ x 11 inches in size and maximum allowable size is 11 x 14 inches. Posters advertising an all-University event should be 17 x 21 inches, and the maximum allowed is set at 22 x 28 inches.

C. <u>Selective Service Information.</u> All requests for information to be sent to Selective Service local boards are handled by the office of Admissions and Records.

At the close of each regular semester a scholastic rank in class is determined for all male students completing an academic year at that time. Students who wish to be considered for an educational deferment should complete a Selective Service record card at Room 15, Window E. This sets up a permanent file, and the student's local board is notified of full-time attendance, scholastic rank in class, and all other information affecting his draft status. Students also may bring to this office any problems concerning their personal draft status.

special regulations

56. Lockers

A total of 3500 lockers are available for students at the Chicago Undergraduate Division. Students receive locker assignments upon presentation of the Student Identification Card at the completion of their registration each semester. Lockers are assigned at each registration period and no locker is retained more than one semester.

Lockers must be vacated the second day following the final examination period each semester. Articles left in lockers after that date are held for 30 days at the police office, and then disposed of. The University is not responsible for any articles left in the lockers.

57. Lost and Found

Articles found should be turned in to the Lost and Found department located in the police office in the building west of the Pier. Any article turned in will be kept for 90 days, after which, if it is not claimed, it will be returned to the finder. A list of articles turned in is posted on the bulletin boards monthly.

58. Smoking

University regulations prohibit smoking in areas designated by "NO SMOKING" signs. Smoking is not permitted in any classroom or laboratory area at any time, nor in the second floor classroom area. Areas in which smoking is permitted are (a) administration building, (b) lounges, snack bars, and cafeterias, (c) staff offices, (d) locker areas, (e) toilets, and (f) first floor corridor.

59. Swimming Regulations

Swimming off Navy Pier is dangerous due to underwater obstructions, strong undertow, and absence of life guards. Swimming off the Pier is therefore prohibited except under the direct supervision of the Physical Education department.

60. Hitchhiking

Soliciting of rides on Lake Shore Drive or any of the parkways is a violation of the Chicago Park District ordinances. Violation of these ordinances will result in prosecution by city law enforcement authorities.

61. Concessions

Under the provisions of the University of Illinois lease with the City of Chicago, concessions are prohibited on all property at Navy Pier which is rented by the University.

62. Building Security

All outside doors are secured at 7 p.m. Monday through Friday, except the main entrance and the entrance at Frame 93. Saturday, Sundays, and holidays all doors are secured, except the main entrance.

Entrance doors at Frame 93 will be secured at 11:50 p.m. Monday through Friday, except that when some activity is held at the east end of the Pier this entrance will be open until such time as the activity is over and all people are clear of the building.

No one will be admitted to the building after the above hours without a Chicago Undergraduate Division building pass or a University of Illinois "Official" badge.

Arrangements must be made with the Physical Plant department to have the building open for all group activities held on the campus after hours.

63. Handbills

No student organization or student acting independently or in the name of an organization shall distribute handbills or printed notices of any description on the campus unless permission to do so has been granted by the Dean of Students.

64. Student Identification Cards

Identification cards are to be available at all times upon call of University officials.

65. Student Conduct

The University expects students to observe the highest standards of cleanliness and sanitation and to use due care in using University facilities. Misuse of furniture and defacing of walls will not be tolerated.

66. Discipline

   A. Basis for Discipline. The University reserves the right to exclude at any time students whose conduct is deemed undesirable or prejudicial to the University's best interest, examples of which, without excluding others, are gambling, violations of law involving moral turpitude, intoxication, and disorderly conduct. Students may be subject to discipline for other sufficient cause, including repeated absences from classes, failure to withdraw properly, and failure to respond to official correspondence.

   B. Administration of Discipline. Discipline is administered through the Senate Committee on Discipline and the Chicago Undergraduate Sub-Committee. The Sub-Committee has original jurisdiction to hear the evidence and take action in all disciplinary cases. The Senate Committee on Discipline hears cases appealed to it.

67. Solicitations

   A. General solicitations or drives for funds shall be permitted in University buildings only if approved by the office of the Dean. If such approval is obtained, all administrative officers and heads of departments will be notified. Otherwise, such activities will be prohibited.

   B. Salesmen, agents, etc., are prohibited on University property except on University business.

68. Student Activities and Organizations

   A. Purpose and Objectives. The University endeavors to provide a well-rounded education by supplementing the student's formal education with opportunities to participate in activities and organizations conducted outside of the classroom. Student enterprises are numerous and varied so that every student has ample opportunity to participate in some creative activity and, if well planned, will help round out a student's life by providing diversified recreation, an outlet for special abilities, and an opportunity to develop the qualities of leadership.

B. <u>Committee on Student Affairs</u>. The Committee on Student Affairs is the official University committee appointed by the Dean of the Undergraduate Division to assist the Dean of Students in the development and supervision of student organizations and student activities. The committee is composed of students, faculty members, and administrative personnel.

C. <u>Directory of Organization</u>. The organizations listed below and on following pages have University recognition and all are fairly active. Generally speaking, the names of these organizations are somewhat self-explanatory as to their aims and objectives. Questions regarding membership in any of these organizations should be directed to the Dean of Students, or to the faculty members who may be sponsors of such organizations, or to the officers of the organizations.

1) <u>Activities Honorary Society</u>. To promote and honor participation in extra-curricular activities.

2) <u>Alpha Lambda Delta</u>. To promote scholarship among women of the freshman class.

3) <u>Amateur Radio Club</u>. To promote interest in amateur radio communication.

4) <u>American Institute of Architects</u>. To provide orientation in the field of architecture.

5) <u>American Institute of Chemical Engineers</u>. To provide orientation in the field of chemistry.

6) <u>American Institute of Electrical Engineers-Institute of Radio Engineers</u>. To provide orientation in the field of electrical and radio engineering.

7) <u>American Society of Civil Engineers</u>. To provide orientation in the field of civil engineering.

8) <u>American Society of Mechanical Engineers</u>. To provide orientation in the field of mechanics.

9) <u>Biology Club</u>. To foster, encourage, and develop an active interest in biological sciences.

10) <u>Cadet Association</u>. To conduct extra-curricular activities for ROTC on campus.

11) <u>Cheerleaders</u>. To promote school spirit.

12) <u>Chess Club</u>. To improve skill and foster competition.

13) <u>Chi A_1ph_a Pi</u>. To establish and maintain a rapport between pre- and post-nursing students.

14) <u>Commerce Club</u>. To promote interest in commerce.

15) <u>Co-Recreational Association</u>. To encourage sports between men and women.

16) <u>French Club</u>. To promote interest in language and culture.

17) <u>Future Teachers of America</u>. To develop among young people preparing to be teachers an organization which shall be an integral part of state and national education associations.

18) <u>Geology Club</u>. To acquaint students with the various aspects of geology.

19) <u>German Club</u>. To promote interest in language and culture.

20) <u>Humanities Club</u>. To encourage the discussion of the humanities and all related subjects, and to further an appreciation of the arts among the student body and faculty.

21) <u>Illinois Technograph</u>. To promote interest in engineering societies.

22) **Institute of Aeronautical Sciences.** To provide orientation in the art or science of operating aircraft.

23) **International Relations Club.** To promote interest in world affairs and current events.

24) **Music Appreciation Club.** To promote interest in the understanding and appreciation of music.

25) **Omega Beta Pi.** To promote scholarship among pre-medical students.

26) **Orchesis.** To give students an opportunity for creative dance study, composition and performance.

27) **Pershing Rifles.** To develop the highest of ideals in the military profession.

28) **Phi Eta Sigma.** To promote scholarship among the male members of the freshman class.

29) **Physical Education Majors.** To promote professional co-operation and practices in the field of health, physical education, and recreation.

30) **Pier Illini.** To provide an outlet for students interested in journalism.

31) **Pier Playhouse.** To promote interest in dramatic skills.

32) **Society of American Military Engineers.** To promote professional and social intercourse.

33) **Society of Mining and Metallurgical Engineers.** To promote professional growth among students of mining and metallurgical engineering.

34) **Spanish Club.** To promote interest in language and culture.

35) **Square Dance Club.** To teach, and offer enjoyment to, students interested in square and folk dancing; to promote this type of dancing as a form of recreation.

36) Student Congress. To promote the general welfare of the student body and encourage extra-curricular activities.

37) Student Engineering Societies Council. To promote interest in engineering.

38) University Band. To encourage students interested in instrumental music and to promote school morale.

39) University Choir. To promote instruction in, and enjoyment of, choral music.

40) University Dance Committee. To promote University dances.

41) Varsity Lettermen's Club. To encourage participation in athletic, scholastic, and social activities.

42) Vets Illini. To organize veterans at school and keep members informed about veterans' rights and benefits, to provide assistance by veterans to other members who are having difficulties resuming studies, and to support and augment student activities.

43) Women's Athletic Association. To encourage athletics.

D. Recognition. Groups of students with common interests who wish to petition for recognition as a organization may do so by contacting the Office of the Dean of Students for the necessary forms and instructions on the procedure to follow for recognition. Students are encouraged to have a preliminary consultation with the Dean of Students during the formative period of organization, at which time detailed information and instructions will be given out. At this time permission to use University space for an organization meeting should be obtained, and approval of the use of the school newspaper and bulletin boards to announce this meeting should be secured. At this organization meeting, the necessary information can be assembled to make out the formal petition for recognition.

Information required for filing a petition with the Dean of Students for recognition of an organization is as follows:

1) Statement of the purpose and function.
2) Signatures of 25 interested students or sufficient number to manifest an adequate interest.
3) Names of one or more faculty members interested and willing to serve as sponsor.
4) Names of the temporary officers.
5) Statement of the requirements for membership.
6) Information regarding initiation fee and/or dues.
7) Copy of the constitution and by-laws.

Succeeding steps in the recognition are as follows:

a) The petition is forwarded by the Dean of Students to the Committee on Student Affairs and the Student Congress.
b) The petition is then forwarded to the chairman of the appropriate administrative committee. The temporary president of the organization may contact the chairman and/or student members of this committee to further the process of recognition.
c) Recommendations as to recognition or non-recognition are made by the administrative committee to the Committee on Student Affairs and the Student Congress.
d) The chairman recommends to the Committee the sponsor to be named from a list of three nominated by the students.
e) Favorable action by the Committee accords probationary recognition for six months. At the end

of this period full recognition is automatically given unless specifically denied by the Committee.

f) Recognized groups must report at once any officer changes.

E. Special Events and Social Functions. Special events or social functions given by or for a group of students or an organization at which men and women students are present may be held only with formal permission from the Dean of Students and the Committee on Student Affairs. Petitions to hold special events or social functions, along with tentative budgets, must be filed in duplicate with the Dean of Students at least one month in advance of the date of the function. Petition blanks and budget blanks are available in the Dean of Students office.

The proposed time and place of all special events or social functions must be cleared and scheduled tentatively on the school activities calendar with the Dean of Women before complete arrangements are made. Consult the Dean of Men concerning financial details before definite and final arrangements are made regarding tickets, contracts let, invitations issued, or publicity released. During this conference the possible need for a number to be punched on the I.D. card as a basis for admission or other valued purposes will be requested.

Each social function must have two or more faculty and staff couples, one of whom is the organization's sponsor, as chaperones in attendance during the hours of any social event. Married couples are preferable and one of the family must be a member of the faculty or staff of the University. The names of chaperones must be designated on the petition. The office of the Dean of Women will forward chaperone cards to the faculty members. They will be required to file and report on the function to the Dean of Women within one week after the event.

The sponsoring group will be required to file a final report on the special event or social function with the Dean of Students within one week after the event.

F. Advisors to Student Organizations. All student clubs or organizations must have a sponsor. A sponsor is the member of the faculty or administrative staff. The approval of a sponsor is by the Committee on Student Affairs from the names of nominees submitted by the student participants. It is the responsibility of the student organization to consider its sponsor as an important and active member of the group, to seek the counsel of its sponsor frequently, and to be fully aware of the sponsor's responsibility for the group and its activities.

It is the responsibility of the sponsor to attend the majority of the meetings of the student organization for which he serves as advisor and counselor, to be active with the group in formulating and executing its policies and activities, and to assist in drawing up a constitution, but not to displace worthy students in the organization, and to see that the activities of the group are in keeping with the purpose of the student organization, and that activities are carried on in a manner which reflects efficient organization and University standards of good taste and conduct.

Other duties of sponsors are as follows:

1) Oversee elections of officers and establish responsibility of each in the constitutions.

2) Pass upon and sign all petitions for special events, including budget.

3) Approve or disapprove organization's request for the expenditure of money.

4) Contact the chairman of the committee under which the organization operates in reference to all major problems.

5) Check the treasurer's accounts, property inventory lists, and custody of any University keys, periodically.

6) Together with the president of the organization, submit to the Dean of Students an annual report, before May 20, covering the year's operations and any recommendations for future operations. Financial status, property inventory, and the return of keys to Physical Plant should be included.

7) It is important that sponsors deny a student participation in an organization's activities if such participation adversely affects his curricular work.

Sponsors serve for one year commencing with the fall semester. Re-appointment for succeeding years will be automatic unless the organization or the sponsor requests a change. Such a request, when necessary, should be directed to the Dean of Students. When the request comes from an organization, it will be considered only on the basis of desires expressed by a majority vote of the total membership of the entire group.

Co-sponsors selected by the sponsor are authorized. (Names of such should be furnished to the Dean of Students and the chairman of the Committee on Student Affairs.)

G. Student Affairs Regulations.

1) Scholastic Probation. Students on scholastic probation are to be governed by the following rules:

a) Students on scholastic probation are not permitted to hold office in any student organization.

b) Students on scholastic probation are not, as a general rule, permitted to participate in extra-curricular activities.

c) Appreciating that under certain circumstances participation in such affairs might add, rather than detract, from a student's ability to meet an academic program, participation may be permitted provided that written permission to do so has been secured from the dean of his college.

2) Events and Final Exams. No special events or social functions may be held during a final examination period. Permission to hold such events at any time must be obtained from the office of the Dean of Students.

3) Closing Hours. "All-University" events and functions shall close by 1 a.m. "Closed" social functions, sponsored by clubs or organizations and held at the University, shall close no later than 12 midnight.

4) Invitations. The invitation list for all-school social functions and special events shall include the staff members (administrative officers) and the members of the Committee on Student Affairs.

5) Publicity. Publicity for a special event or social function shall not be released until formal approval to hold the event is secured from the Dean of Students and the Committee on Student Affairs. Likewise, invitations shall not be sent or given out until such approval has been granted.

6) Major-Minor Offices. No student may hold more than one major office or two minor offices at the same time. For definitions of major and minor, see Section H following.

7) Solicitation of Funds. No student organization, or student acting in the name of an organization,

shall solicit or receive contributions from persons outside of the organization's own membership for any purpose, unless permission to do so has been granted previously by the Dean of Students and the Committee on Student Affairs.

8) Awards. A certificate entitled "Award of Excellence" will be awarded, at the close of the school year, to not over 10 per cent of an organization's membership upon recommendation of the advisor to the Dean of Students.

9) Off Campus Speakers. Applications for permission to invite off campus speakers (not connected with other divisions of the University) must be made to the Dean of Students at least two weeks in advance, and before announcements are made or invitations are extended.

10) Room Keys. Organizations having a permanent room assignment will obtain a key for the room through a request from the sponsor to the Dean of Students. On approval of the sponsor, the Dean of Students will issue the official key card request in the name of the student for the organization, who shall sign for the key to be issued at the Physical Plant department, Room 158. All keys are to be returned to the Physical Plant department at the close of the spring semester each year or when the organization no longer needs the room.

11) Bulletin Boards. Physical Plant is charged with the installation and general appearance of all bulletin boards. Certain of these are reserved for student organizations publicity. Before such material is posted, the student shall deliver same to the Dean of Students office whereby the approved stamp of the Dean of Students office may be applied to the material and forwarded to the Physical Plant department for posting in the

glass-covered student activities bulletin boards. The individual departments bulletin boards usually located on the wall immediately outside of the doorway to the department are not to be used for student activities unless approved by the department concerned.

12) Payment on Acceptance of Gratuities. Organizations such as student publications, bands, orchestra, and choir, which receive major financial support from allocations from the Student Activities Fee fund, are not authorized to accept pay or gratuities in behalf of the organization or for individual members participating in any authorized performance.

13) Reimbursement for Expenses. The Committee on Student Affairs will give every consideration to reimbursing students for personal expenses such as travel expenses and damage to private equipment and instruments incurred in authorized performances and regularly scheduled rehearsals.

14) Use of Rooms. Permission must be obtained from the office of the Dean of Students for the use of any University room or space for extracurricular activities sponsored by students at any time.

15) Use of Auditorium. All requests for the use of the Auditorium should be directed to the Director of Physical Education. Once permission is granted, a room reservation form should be obtained, completed and returned to the Dean of Student's office.

16) Physical Plant Services. Requests by organizations for work to be done by the Physical Plant department must be made (requisitions) through the Dean of Men's office at least three full days in advance.

17) Building Security. All outside doors are secured at 7 p.m. Monday through Friday, except the main entrance and the entrance at Frame 93. Saturdays, Sundays and holidays all doors are secured except the main entrance. No one will be admitted to the building after the above hours without a Chicago Undergraduate Division building pass or a University of Illinois "Official" badge.

Arrangements must be made with the Physical Plant department to have the building open for all group activities held on the campus after hours.

18) Alterations. Student organizations are not permitted to make alterations or extensions to any public service lines. Physical Plant will do all such work, if necessary, at the expense of the student organization requesting it.

19) Fireproof Decorations. All decorations shall be fireproofed in accordance with Physical Plant specifications.

H. Definitions

1) Activity Hour. The period from 1 to 2 p.m. (1 p.m. to 1:50 p.m., actually) is reserved for activities on Tuesday of each week, and on the second and fourth Thursdays of each month. (The first and third Thursdays of each month are reserved for all-University convocations.)

2) All-University Event. Any extra-curricular event open to all students.

3) Closed Functions. Any extra-curricular event open only to the membership of the organization.

4) Special Events. Any event planned by a single organization or a combination of clubs or organizations which goes beyond the basic purposes of

the clubs or organization, and which require special planning and committee assignments.

5) **Major Office.** Major student office is defined as president, vice president, secretary, or treasurer of the Student Congress, and president of any club or organization.

6) **Minor Office.** Minor student office is defined as any office, except presidency or chairmanship of a permanent committee of a club or organization. Student Congress representatives are also considered as holding a minor office.

index

	Paragraph
Activities and Organizations	68
Recognition	68D
Advisors	68F
Absences	33
Address Change	8
Admission to Professional Colleges	15
Advisement, Pre-registration	25
Alteration of Records	21
Books and Supplies, Veterans	42
Bookstore	53
Building Security	62
Bulletin Boards	55B
Changes, Address or Name	8
Colleges within the Chicago Undergraduate Division	14
Curriculum within Colleges	13
Educational Objective, Veterans	46
Subjects or Sections	12
College Credit for High School Courses	11
Colleges, How to Change	14
Commerce and Business Administration, Scholastic Requirements	27A
Concessions	61

INDEX - Continued

	Paragraph
Conduct	65
Correspondence Courses	30
Counseling Bureau	50
Dean of Students	47
Discipline	66
Employment	49C
Engineering Sciences, Scholastic Requirements	27B
English Requirements	31
Examinations, Proficiency	32B
Semester	32A
Special	32C
Fees	4
Indebtedness	4B
Late Registration	4C
Refunds	5
When Payable	4A
Food Service	54
General Deposit, Rebate	5B
Grades, Mid-term Reports	28D
Semester Reports	6
Significance	28A
Transcripts	7
Graduation Requirements	23
Residence	24

INDEX - Continued

	Paragraph
Scholastic	26C
Handbills	63
Health	48
Honors	28B
Honoraries, Scholastic	28C
Hospital and Medical Insurance	48B
Rebate of Fee	5A
Hygiene	36
Identification Cards	64
Library Records	52B
Information Records	55
Liberal Arts and Sciences, Scholastic Requirements	27C
Library Services	52
Loan Funds	49B
Lockers	56
Lost and Found	57
Military Science	35
Deposit	5C
Name Change	8
Physical Education Requirements	34
Physical Education, Scholastic Requirements	27D
Pre-registration Advisement	25
Probation	26A
Professional Colleges, Admission	15

72

INDEX - Continued

	Paragraph
Proficiency Examinations	32B
Re-admission to the University	20
Refunds of Fees	5
Registration, Days	1
Late	2
Listeners or Visitors	3
Pre-registration Advisement	25
Repeating a Course	29
Repetition of Courses Taken in High School	9
Selective Service Information	55C
Scholastic Honoraries	28C
Scholastic Requirements	26
Commerce and Business Administration	27A
Engineering Sciences	27B
Liberal Arts and Sciences	27C
Physical Education	27D
Probation	26A
Student Affairs Regulations	68G
Veterans	44
Scholarships	49
Smoking	58
Solicitations	67
Speech Correction	51
Special Events and Social Functions	68E
Special Examinations	32C

INDEX - Continued

	Paragraph
Subjects or Sections, How to Change	12
Training Records, Veterans	37
Transcripts	7
Transfers, Inter-college	14
Other Institutions	17
Urbana	16
Veterans	45
Veterans, Counselor	38
Illinois Commission	39
Records	37
Welfare	48
Withdrawal from the University	18
To Enter Armed Forces	19
Veterans	43